Sanctus, Sanctus, Sanctus

An Introductory Latin Missal for Children

Illustrated by Adalee Hude

Text: "New Roman Missal Lasance English/Latin," 1937 and
"The Roman Missal: Translated into the English Language for the use of the Laity.
To which is Prefixed, an Historical Explanation of the Vestments, Ceremonies, Etc.," 1843.

Book Design by Adalee Hude.
ISBN: 978-1-5051-2829-1 | Kindle ISBN: 978-1-5051-2830-7 |
ePUB ISBN: 978-1-5051-2831-4
Published in the United States by
TAN Books . PO Box 269 . Gastonia, NC, 28053
www.TANBooks.com
Printed in India

-For all of those who love,
and are learning to love,
the Traditional Roman Rite.

Cope

V. Osténde nobis, Dómine, misericórdiam tuam.
R. Et salutáre tuum da nobis.
V. Dómine exáudi oratiónem meam.
R. Et clamor meus ad te véniat.

Aspérges Me, Dómine, hyssópo, et mundábor: lavábis me, et super nivem dealbábor.

P. Misérere Mei, Deus, secúndum magnam misericórdiam tuam. V. Gloria Patri...

- In Pascha -

Vidi Aquam egrediéntem de templo, a látere dextro, allelúia: et omnes ad quos pervénit aqua ista salvi facti sunt, et dicent, allelúia.

V: DÓMINUS VOBÍSCUM.

R. Et cum spíritu tuo.

℣. Show us, O Lord, Thy mercy.
℟. And grant us Thy salvation.
℣. O Lord, hear my prayer.
℟. And let my cry come unto Thee.

Thou shalt sprinkle me, O Lord, with hyssop, and I shall be cleansed: Thou shalt wash me and I shall be made whiter than snow.

P. Have mercy on me,
O God, according to Thy great mercy.
V. Glory be to the Father...

- In Easter -

I saw water coming forth from the temple on the right side, alleluia: and all those to whom this water came, were saved, and shall say, alleluia.

℣: THE LORD BE WITH YOU.

℟. And with thy spirit.

P. IN NÓMINE PATRIS,
✠ et Fílii, et Spíritus Sancti. Amen.

P. Introíbo ad altáre Dei.
℟. Ad Deum, qui lætíficat iuventútem meam.

P. IÚDICA me, Deus, et discérne causam meam de gente non sancta: ab hómine iníquo et dolóso érue me….

P.Adiutórium nostrum ✠ in nómine Dómini.
℟. Qui fecit coelum et terram....

❖

IN THE NAME OF THE FATHER,
✠ and of the Son, and of the Holy Ghost...

P. I will go in to the altar of God.
℟. To God, Who giveth joy to my youth.

P. JUDGE ME, O God, and distinguish my cause from the nation that is not holy; deliver me from the unjust and deceitful man….

P. Our help ✠ is in the name of the Lord.
℟. Who made Heaven and earth....

CONFÍTEOR Deo
omnipoténti, beátæ Maríæ
semper Vírgini, beáto Michaéli
archángelo, beáto Joánni Baptístæ,
sanctis Apóstolis Petro et Paulo,
ómnibus Sanctis, et tibi Pater quia
peccávi nimis cogitatióne, verbo et opere:
mea culpa, mea culpa, mea máxima culpa.
Ideo precor beátam Maríam semper Vírginem, beátum Michaélem Archángelum, beátum Joánnem Baptístam, sanctos Apóstolos Petrum et Paulum, omnes Sanctos, et te, Pater
orare pro me ad Dóminum, Deum nostrum.

❖

I CONFESS to Almighty God, to blessed Mary ever Virgin, to blessed Michael the Archangel, to blessed John the Baptist, to the holy apostle Peter and Paul, to all the saints, and to you, Father, that I have sinned exceedingly, in thought, word, and deed: through my fault, through my fault, through my most grievous fault. Therefore I beseech the Blessed Mary, ever a virgin, Blessed Michael the Archangel, Blessed John the Baptist, the holy Apostles Peter and Paul, and all the Saints, and you, O Father, to pray to the Lord our God for me.

Orémus.... ✠

AUFER a nobis, quæsumus, Dómine,
iniquitátes nostras....
ORÁMUS te Dómine, per mérita Sanctorum tuórum....
AB illo ✠ benedicáris in cujus honore cremáberis. Amen

P. Kýrie, eléison. ℟. Kýrie, eléison.
P. Kýrie, eléison.

℟. Christe, eléison. P. Christe, eléison.
℟. Christe, eléison.

P. Kýrie, eléison. ℟. Kýrie, eléison.

P. Kýrie, eléison.

❖

Let us pray.... ✠

TAKE away from us our iniquities....
WE beseech thee O Lord by the merits of those of thy saints....
MAYEST thou be ✠ blessed by Him in Whose honor
thou shalt be burnt. Amen.

P. Lord, have mercy on us. ℟. Lord, have mercy on us.
P. Lord, have mercy on us.

℟. Christ, have mercy on us. P. Christ, have mercy on us.
℟. Christ, have mercy on us.

P. Lord, have mercy on us. ℟. Lord, have mercy on us.
P. Lord, have mercy on us.

GLÓRIA
in excélsis Deo,
et in terra pax homínibus
bonæ voluntátis.

Laudámus te, benedícimus te,
adorámus te,
glorificámus te. Grátias ágimus tibi
propter magnam glóriam tuam.

Dómine Deus rex coeléstis,
Deus Pater omnípotens. Dómine Fili
unigénite, Jesu Christe. Dómine Deus,
Agnus Dei, Fílius Patris.

Qui tollis peccáta mundi, miserére nobis.
Qui tollis peccáta mundi, súscipe
deprecatiónem nostram. Qui sedes ad
déxteram Patris, miserére nobis.

Quóniam tu solus Sanctus,
tu solus Dóminus,
tu solus altíssimus, Jesu Christe,
cum Sancto Spíritu
in glória Dei Patris.

Amen.

GLORY be to God on high, and on earth
peace to men of good will.

We praise Thee; we bless Thee;
we adore Thee; we glorify Thee.
We give Thee thanks for Thy great glory.

O Lord God, heavenly king,
God the Father almighty,
O Lord Jesus Christ, the only-begotten Son.
O Lord God, Lamb of God,
Son of the Father.

Who takest away the sins of the world,
have mercy on us.
Who takest away the sins of the world,
receive our prayer.
Who sittest at the right hand of the Father,
have mercy on us.

For Thou alone art holy;
Thou alone art the Lord;
Thou alone, O Jesus Christ,
together with the Holy Ghost,
art most high in the
glory of God the Father.

Amen.

COLLECT

P. Orémus. Omnípotens sempitérne Deus....
℟. Amen.

EPISTOLÆ

P. Léctio Epistolæ beáti....
℟. Deo gratias.

❖

COLLECT

P. Let us pray. O Almighty and
Everlasting God....
℟. Amen.

EPISTLE

P. A Lesson from the Epistle of St....
℟. Thanks be to God.

MUNDA cor meum ac labia mea....
DÓMINUS sit in corde meo et in lábiis meis: ut digne… annúntiem Evangélium suum.
Amen.

P. Dóminus vobíscum.
℟. Et cum spiritu tuo.
P. Sequentia sancti Evangelii secundum....
℟. Gloria tibi, Domine.
...
℟. Laus tibi, Christe.
P. Per evangélica dicta,
deleántur nostra delícta.

❖

CLEANSE my heart and my lips....
MAY the Lord be in my heart and on my lips that I may worthily… attend to His holy Gospel.
Amen.

P. The Lord be with you.
℟. And with thy spirit.
P. The continuation of the holy Gospel according to....
℟. Glory to Thee, O Lord.
...
℟. Praise be to Thee, O Christ.
P. May our sins be blotted out by the words of the Gospel.

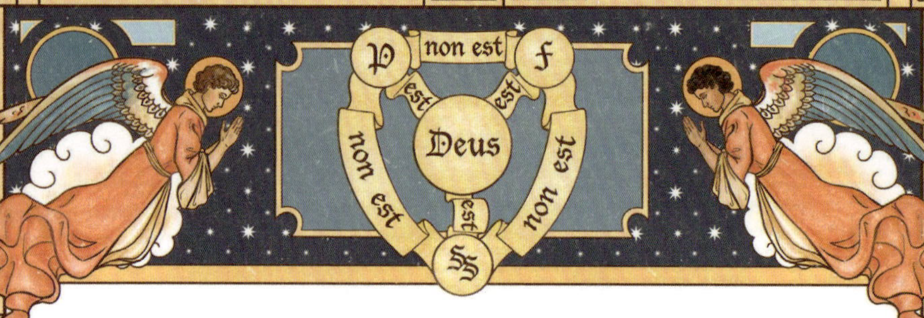

CREDO in unum Deum, Patrem omnipoténtem, factórem cæli et terræ, visibílium ómnium et in visibílium. Et in unum Dóminum Jesum Christum, Fílium Dei unigénitum. Et ex Patre natum ante ómnia sæcula. Deum de Deo, lumen de lúmine, Deum verum de Deo vero. Génitum, non factum, consubstantiálem Patri: per quem ómnia facta sunt. Qui propter nos hómines et propter nostram salútem descéndit de cælis.

ET INCARNÁTUS EST DE SPÍRITU SANCTO EX MARÍA VÍRGINE: ET HOMO FACTUS EST.

Crucifíxus étiam pro nobis: sub Póntio Piláto passus, et sepúltus est. Et resurréxit tértia die, secúndum Scriptúras. Et ascéndit in cælum: sedet ad déxteram Patris. Et íterum ventúrus est cum glória iudicáre vivos et mórtuos: cuius regni non erit finis. Et in Spíritum Sanctum, Dóminum et vivificántem: qui ex Patre Filióque procédit. Qui cum Patre et Fílio simul adorátur et conglorificátur: qui locútus est per Prophétas. Et unam sanctam cathólicam et apostólicam Ecclésiam. Confíteor unum baptísma in remissiónem peccatórum. Et exspécto resurrectiónem mortuórum. Et vitam ✠ ventúri sæculi. Amen.

I BELIEVE in one God, the Father Almighty,
Maker of heaven and earth, and of all things visible and invisible.
And in one Lord Jesus Christ, the only begotten son of God,
and born of the Father before all ages. God of God;
Light of Light, true God of true God: Begotten not made:
consubstantial to the Father, by Whom all things were made.
For Who us men, and for our salvation, came down from heaven,

AND BECAME INCARNATE BY THE HOLY GHOST OF THE VIRGIN MARY: AND WAS MADE MAN.

He was crucified also for us, suffered under Pontius Pilate, and was buried. And the third day He arose again, according to the Scriptures. He ascended into heaven. He sitteth at the right hand of the Father: and He shall come again in glory to judge the living and the dead: and His kingdom will have no end. And in the Holy Ghost, the Lord and Giver of life, Who proceedeth from the Father and the Son, Who, together with the Father and the Son, is adored and glorified: Who spoke through the Prophets. And one holy Catholic and apostolic Church. I confess one baptism for the forgiveness of sins. And I expect the resurrection of the dead, and the life ✠ of the world to come. Amen.

SÚSCIPE Sancte Pater omnipotens ætérne Deus,
hanc immaculátam hóstiam….
DEUS, qui humánæ substántiae…
OFFÉRIMUS tibi Dómine, cálicem salutáris,
tuam deprecántes cleméntiam....
IN spíritu humilitátis et in ánimo contrito…
VENI, sanctificátor omnípotens ætérne Deus….
LAVÁBO inter innocéntes manus meas....
SÚSCIPE Sancta Trinítas hanc oblatiónem, quam tibi offérimus...
ORÁTE, fratres, ut meum ac vestrum sacrifícium acceptábile
fiat apud Deum Patrem omnipoténtem.

P. Per ómnia sæcula sæculórum. ℟. Amen P. Dóminus
vobíscum. ℟. Et cum spíritu tuo. P. Sursum corda.
℟. Habémus ad Dóminum. P. Grátias agámus Dómino
Deo nostro. ℟. Dignum et iustum est.

❖

RECEIVE, O Holy Father, almighty and eternal God,
this spotless host….
O GOD, Who in creating man…
WE OFFER unto Thee, O Lord, the chalice of salvation,
beseeching Thy clemency....
HUMBLED in mind, contrite of heart…
COME, Thou the Sanctifier, God almighty and everlasting….
I WILL WASH MY HANDS among the innocent....
RECEIVE, O HOLY TRINITY, this oblation
offered up by us to Thee...
BRETHREN, PRAY that my Sacrifice and yours
may be well pleasing to God the Father Almighty.

P. World without end. ℟ Amen.
P. The Lord be with you. ℟. And with thy spirit.
P. Lift up your hearts. ℟. We have them lifted up unto the Lord.
P. Let us give thanks to the Lord our God.
℟. It is meet and just.

Per intercessiónem beáti Michǽlis Archángeli.... Incénsum istud a te benedíctum.... Dirigátur,
dómine orátio mea, sicut in-cénsum.... Accéndat in nob
is Dóminus ignem sui amóris.... May the Lord, by the intercession of blessed Michael the Arch
angel.... May this incense which Thou hast blessed....

Sanctus
HOLY
Sanctus
HOLY
Sanctus
HOLY
Te Igitur...
Meménto, Dómine...
Communicántes...
Hanc Igitur...
PLENÍ SUNT CÆLI ET TERRA GLÓRIA TUA.
HOSÁNNA IN EXCELSIS. ✠ BENEDICTUS QUI VENIT IN NOMINE DÓMINI.
HOSÁNNA IN EXCELSIS.

Dóminus
LORD
Deus
GOD OF
Sabaoth
HOSTS
Wherefore ...
Be Mindful, O Lord...
Having Communion...
Wherefore ...
HEAVENS AND THE EARTH ART FULL
OF THY GLORY. HOSANA IN THE HIGHEST.
✠ BLESSED IS HE WHO COMES
IN THE NAME OF THE LORD.
HOSANA IN THE HIGHEST.

QUAM oblatiónem tu,
Deus, in ómnibus, quæsumus,
bene ✠ díctam,
adscríp ✠ tam, ra ✠ tam,
rationábilem, acceptabilémque fácere
dignéris: ut nobis Cor ✠ pus, et
San ✠ guis fiat dilectíssimi Fílii tui
Dómini nostri Jesu Christe.

QUI prídie quam paterétur, accépit
panem in sanctas ac venerábiles manus
suas, et elevátis óculis in coelum ad te
Deum, Patrem suum omnipoténtem,
tibi grátias agens, bene ✠ dixit, fregit,
dedítque discípulis suis, dicens:
Accípite, et manducáte ex hoc omnes:

HOC EST ENIM CORPUS MEUM.

AND DO THOU,
O God, vouchsafe in all respects to bless ✠, to consecrate ✠ and approve ✠ this our oblation, to perfect it, and to render it well pleasing to Thyself, so that it may become for us the Body ✠ and Blood ✠ of Thy most beloved Son, Jesus Christ our Lord.

WHO, the day before He suffered took bread into His Holy and venerable hands, and having lifted up His eyes to heaven, to Thee, God, His almighty Father, giving thanks to Thee, blessed it ✠, broke it, and gave it to His disciples, saying:
Take ye and eat ye all of this.

FOR THIS IS MY BODY.

SÍMILI modo postquam cænátum est, accípiens et hunc præclárum Cálicem in sanctas ac venerábiles manus suas: item tibi grátias agens, bene ✠ dixit, dedítque discípulis suis, dicens: Accípite, et bíbite ex eo omnes.

HIC EST ENIM CALIX SÁNGUINIS MEI, NOVI ET ÆTÉRNI TESTAMÉNTI: MYSTÉRIUM FÍDEI: QUI PRO VOBIS ET PRO MULTIS EFFUNDÉTUR IN REMISSIÓNEM PECCATÓRUM.

❖

IN like manner, after He had supped, taking also into His holy and venerable hands this goodly chalice, again giving thanks to Thee, He blessed it, ✠ and gave it to His disciples, saying: Take ye and drink ye all of this.

FOR THIS IS THE CHALICE OF MY BLOOD, OF THE NEW AND EVERLASTING TESTAMENT, THE MYSTERY OF FAITH, WHICH FOR YOU AND FOR MANY SHALL BE SHED UNTO THE REMISSION OF SINS.

UNDE et mémores, Dómine, nos servi tui, sed et plebs tua sancta....

SUPRA quæ propítio ac seréno vultu respícere dignéris: et accépta habére....

SÚPPLICES te rogámus, omnípotens Deus: iube hæc perférri per manus sancti Angeli tui in sublíme altáre tuum, in conspéctu divínæ maiestátis tuæ: ut, quotquot ex hac altáris participatióne sacrosánctum Fílii tui, Cor ✠ pus, et Sán ✠ guinem sumpsérimus, omni benedictióne coelésti et grátia repleámur....

MEMÉNTO étiam, Dómine, famulórum famularúmque tuárum...
qui nos præcessérunt cum signo fídei....

❖

WHEREFORE, O Lord, we, Thy servants, as also Thy holy people....

VOUCHSAFE to look upon them with a gracious and tranquil countenance....

WE HUMBLY beseech Thee, almighty God, to command that these our offerings be borne by the hands of Thy holy angel, to Thine altar on high, in the presence of Thy divine majesty, that as many of us as shall receive the most sacred ✠ body and ✠ blood of Thy Son by partaking thereof from this altar may be filled with every heavenly blessing and grace....

BE MINDFUL, also, O Lord, of Thy servants... who have gone before us....

NOBIS QUOQUE PECCATÓRIBUS fámulis tuis, de multitúdine miseratiónum tuárum sperántibus, partem áliquam et societátem donáre dignéris, cum tuis sanctis Apóstolis et Martýribus....

PER quem hæc ómnia, Dómine, semper bona creas, sancti ✠ ficas, viví ✠ ficas, bene ✠ dícis et præstas nobis.

PER IP ✠ SUM, ET CUM IP ✠ SO, ET IN IP ✠ SO, est tibi Deo Patri ✠ omnipotenti, in unitáte Spíritus ✠ Sancti, omnis honor, et glória. Per omnia saecula saecolorum. ℟. Amen.

PATER NOSTER, qui es in caelis, Sanctificétur nomen tuum. Advéniat regnum tuum. Fiat vóluntas tua, sicut in coelo et in terra. Panem nostrum quotidiánum da nobis hódie. Et dimítte nobis débita nostra, sicut et nos dimíttimus debitóribus nostris. Et ne nos indúcas in tentatiónem:
℟. Sed libera nos a malo.

TO US SINNERS, also Thy servants, who put our trust in the multitude of Thy mercies, vouchsafe to grant some part and fellowship with Thy holy apostles and martyrs....

BY Whom, O Lord, Thou dost always create, sanctify, ✠ quicken, ✠ bless ✠ and bestow upon us all these good things.

THROUGH HIM ✠, AND WITH HIM ✠, AND IN HIM, ✠, is to Thee, God the Father ✠ almighty, in the unity of the Holy ✠ Ghost, all honor and glory. World without end.

℟. Amen.

OUR FATHER, Who art in heaven, hallowed be Thy Name; Thy kingdom come; Thy will be done on earth as it is in heaven. Give us this day our daily bread; and forgive us our trespasses as we forgive those who trespass against us. And lead us not into temptation. ℟. But deliver us from evil.

Amen.

LÍBERA nos, quaesumus, Dómine, ab ómnibus malis, prætéritis, præséntibus et futúris....

P. Pax ✠ Dómini sit ✠ semper vobís ✠ cum. ℟. Et cum spiritu tuo.

HÆC commíxtio, et consecrátio Córporis et Sánguinis Dómini nostri Iesu Christi, fiat accipiéntibus nobis in vitam ætérnam. Amen.

AGNUS DEI, qui tollis peccáta mundi: miserere nobis. AGNUS DEI, qui tollis peccáta mundi: miserere nobis. Agnus Dei, qui tollis peccáta mundi: dona nobis pacem.

❖

DELIVER us, we beseech Thee, O Lord, from all evils, past, present, and to come....

P. May the peace ✠ of the Lord be ✠ always ✠ with you. ℟. And with thy spirit.

MAY this commingling and consecrating of the Body and Blood of Our Lord Jesus Christ avail us who receive it unto life everlasting. Amen.

LAMB OF GOD, Who takest away the sins of the world, have mercy on us. LAMB OF GOD, Who takest away the sins of the world, have mercy on us. LAMB OF GOD Who takest away the sins of the world, grant us peace.

DÓMINE, NON SUM DIGNIS, UT INTRES SUB TECTUM MEUM: SED TANTUM DIC VERBO, ET SANÁBITUR ÁNIMA MEA. / LORD, I AM NOT WORTHY THAT THOU SHOULDST ENTER UNDER MY ROOF; BUT ONLY SAY THE WORD, AND MY SOUL SHALL BE HEALED.

Ecce Agnus Dei

CORPUS Dómini nostri Iesu Christi custódiat ánimam tuam in vitam ætérnam. Amen.

QUOD ORE SÚMPSIMUS, DÓMINE PURA MENTE CAPIÁMUS....

Behold the Lamb of God

MAY the Body of Our Lord Jesus Christ keep thy soul unto life everlasting. Amen.

GRANT LORD WHAT WE HAVE TAKEN WITH OUR MOUTH WE MAY RECEIVE WITH A PURE MIND....

P. Dóminus vobiscum.
℟. Et cum spíritu tuo.
P. Ite, Missa est.
℟. Deo grátias.

PLÁCEAT tibi, sancta Trínitas, obséquium servitútis meæ: et præsta; ut sacrifícium, quod óculis tuæ maiestátis indígnus óbtuli, tibi sit acceptábile, mihíque et ómnibus, pro quibus illud óbtuli, sit, te miseránte, propitiábile. Per Christum, Dóminum nostrum. Amen.

BENEDÍCAT vos omnípotens Deus, Pater, et Fílius, ✠ et Spíritus Sanctus. ℟. Amen

❖

P. The Lord be with you.
℟. And with thy spirit.
P. Go, the Mass is ended.
℟. Thanks be to God.

MAY the lowly homage of my service be pleasing to Thee. O most holy Trinity: and do Thou grant that the sacrifice which I, all unworthy, have offered up in the sight of Thy majesty, may be acceptable to Thee, and, because of Thy loving-kindness, may avail to atone to Thee for myself and for all those for whom I have offered it up. Through Christ our Lord. Amen.

MAY ALMIGHTY GOD, the Father, Son, ✠ and Holy Ghost, bless you. ℟.Amen.

INRI

Initium Sancti Evangelii secundum Joannem

The beginning of the holy Gospel according to Saint John.

IN princípio erat Verbum, et Verbum erat apud Deum, et Deus erat Verbum. Hoc erat in princípio apud Deum. Omnia per ipsum facta sunt: et sine ipso factum est nihil, quod factum est: in ipso vita erat, et vita erat lux hóminum: et lux in ténebris lucet, et ténebræ eam non comprehendérunt. Fuit homo missus a Deo, cui nomen erat Ioánnes. Hic venit in testimónium, ut testimónium perhibéret de lúmine, ut omnes créderent per illum. Non erat ille lux, sed ut testimónium perhibéret de lúmine. Erat lux vera, quæ illúminat omnem hóminem veniéntem in hunc mundum. In mundo erat, et mundus per ipsum factus est, et mundus eum non cognóvit. In própria venit, et sui eum non recepérunt. Quotquot autem recepérunt eum, dedit eis potestátem fílios Dei fíeri, his, qui credunt in nómine eius: qui non ex sanguínibus, neque ex voluntáte carnis, neque ex voluntáte viri, sed ex Deo nati sunt.

ET VERBUM CARO FACTUM EST

et habitávit in nobis: et vídimus glóriam eius, glóriam quasi Unigéniti a Patre, plenum grátiæ et veritatis.

IN the beginning was the Word, and the Word was with God, and the Word was God. The same was in the beginning with God. All things were made by Him: and without Him was made nothing that was made. In Him was life, and the life was the light of men: and the light shineth in darkness, and the darkness did not comprehend it. There was a man sent from God, Whose name was John. This man came for a witness, to give testimony of the light, that all men might believe through him. He was not the light, but was to give testimony of the light. That was the true light which enlighteneth every man that cometh into this world. He was in the world, and the world was made by Him, and the world knew Him not. He came unto His own, and His own received Him not. But as many as received Him, to them He gave power to become the sons of God, to them that believe in His name. Who are born, not of blood, nor of the will of the flesh, nor of the will of man, but of God.

AND THE WORD WAS MADE FLESH

and dwelt among us, and we saw His glory, the glory as of the only begotten of the Father, full of grace and truth.

Deo Grátias

Thanks be to God